BETTER DAYS ARE COMING

Your New Beginning Awaits

BETTER DAYS ARE COMING

BETTER DAYS ARE COMING

BETTER DAYS ARE COMING

BETTER DAYS ARE COMING

BETTER DAYS ARE COMING

BETTER DAYS ARE COMING

BETTER DAYS ARE COMING

BETTER DAYS ARE COMING

BETTER DAYS ARE COMING

BETTER DAYS ARE COMING

BETTER DAYS ARE COMING

BETTER DAYS ARE COMING

BETTER DAYS ARE COMING

BETTER DAYS ARE COMING

BETTER DAYS ARE COMING

BETTER DAYS ARE COMING

BETTER DAYS ARE COMING

BETTER DAYS ARE COMING

BETTER DAYS ARE COMING

BETTER DAYS ARE COMING

BETTER DAYS ARE COMING

BETTER DAYS ARE COMING

BETTER DAYS ARE COMING

BETTER DAYS ARE COMING

BETTER DAYS ARE COMING

BETTER DAYS ARE COMING

BETTER DAYS ARE COMING

BETTER DAYS ARE COMING

BETTER DAYS ARE COMING

BETTER DAYS ARE COMING

BETTER DAYS ARE COMING

BETTER DAYS ARE COMING

BETTER DAYS ARE COMING

BETTER DAYS ARE COMING

BETTER DAYS ARE COMING

BETTER DAYS ARE COMING

BETTER DAYS ARE COMING

BETTER DAYS ARE COMING

BETTER DAYS ARE COMING

BETTER DAYS ARE COMING

BETTER DAYS ARE COMING

BETTER DAYS ARE COMING

BETTER DAYS ARE COMING

BETTER DAYS ARE COMING

BETTER DAYS ARE COMING

BETTER DAYS ARE COMING

BETTER DAYS ARE COMING

BETTER DAYS ARE COMING

BETTER DAYS ARE COMING

BETTER DAYS ARE COMING

BETTER DAYS ARE COMING

BETTER DAYS ARE COMING

BETTER DAYS ARE COMING

BETTER DAYS ARE COMING

BETTER DAYS ARE COMING

BETTER DAYS ARE COMING

BETTER DAYS ARE COMING

BETTER DAYS ARE COMING

BETTER DAYS ARE COMING

BETTER DAYS ARE COMING

BETTER DAYS ARE COMING

BETTER DAYS ARE COMING

BETTER DAYS ARE COMING

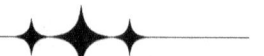

BETTER DAYS ARE COMING

BETTER DAYS ARE COMING

BETTER DAYS ARE COMING

BETTER DAYS ARE COMING

BETTER DAYS ARE COMING

BETTER DAYS ARE COMING

BETTER DAYS ARE COMING

BETTER DAYS ARE COMING

BETTER DAYS ARE COMING

BETTER DAYS ARE COMING

BETTER DAYS ARE COMING

BETTER DAYS ARE COMING

BETTER DAYS ARE COMING

BETTER DAYS ARE COMING

BETTER DAYS ARE COMING

BETTER DAYS ARE COMING

BETTER DAYS ARE COMING

BETTER DAYS ARE COMING

BETTER DAYS ARE COMING

BETTER DAYS ARE COMING

BETTER DAYS ARE COMING

BETTER DAYS ARE COMING

BETTER DAYS ARE COMING

BETTER DAYS ARE COMING

BETTER DAYS ARE COMING

BETTER DAYS ARE COMING

BETTER DAYS ARE COMING

BETTER DAYS ARE COMING

BETTER DAYS ARE COMING

BETTER DAYS ARE COMING

BETTER DAYS ARE COMING

BETTER DAYS ARE COMING

BETTER DAYS ARE COMING

BETTER DAYS ARE COMING

BETTER DAYS ARE COMING

BETTER DAYS ARE COMING

BETTER DAYS ARE COMING

BETTER DAYS ARE COMING

BETTER DAYS ARE COMING

BETTER DAYS ARE COMING

BETTER DAYS ARE COMING

BETTER DAYS ARE COMING

BETTER DAYS ARE COMING

BETTER DAYS ARE COMING

BETTER DAYS ARE COMING

BETTER DAYS ARE COMING

BETTER DAYS ARE COMING

BETTER DAYS ARE COMING

BETTER DAYS ARE COMING

BETTER DAYS ARE COMING

BETTER DAYS ARE COMING

BETTER DAYS ARE COMING

BETTER DAYS ARE COMING

BETTER DAYS ARE COMING

BETTER DAYS ARE COMING

BETTER DAYS ARE COMING

www.ingramcontent.com/pod-product-compliance
Lightning Source LLC
Chambersburg PA
CBHW071003080526
44587CB00015B/2321